BIG

●

A

Think

Collection

Dr. Robert Anthony

BERKLEY BOOKS, NEW YORK

THINK BIG: A THINK COLLECTION

An Berkley Book / published by arrangement with
Prosper International Trust 4856

PRINTING HISTORY
Berkley trade paperback edition/ August 1999

The Penguin Putnam Inc. World Wide Web site address is
http://www.penguinputnam.com

ISBN: 0-425-16866-2

BERKLEY®
Berkley Books are published by
The Berkley Publishing Group, a division of Penguin Putnam Inc.,
375 Hudson Street, New York, New York 10014.
BERKLEY and the "B" design are trademarks
belonging to Penguin Putnam Inc.

PRINTED IN THE UNITED STATES OF AMERICA

10 9

No one writes a book alone. I wish
to acknowledge the immeasurable
contribution others have made to
my life by freely sharing their
enlightenment. It is my sincere
desire that you may benefit from
the ideas contained in this book.

THINK

---●---

You can only have two
things in life, Reasons or
Results. Reasons don't count.

_____

If you are constantly being mistreated, you're cooperating with the treatment.

You don't have to be
positive, you just have to be
yourself.

Trying provides two excuses:
an excuse for not Doing,
and an excuse for not
Having.

—————— ● ——————

You cannot control without
being controlled.

The angry people are those
who are most afraid.

There is no way to know
before experiencing.

**What you said is exactly
what you intended to say.**

Some people are willing to
work, only if they can start
at the top and work up.

---- • ----

**The thing we run from is
the thing we run to.**

Consciously or
unconsciously, you always
get what you expect.

Others can stop you
temporarily, only you can do
it permanently.

---•---

Whatever you are trying to avoid won't go away until you confront it.

———————

Most of our lives are about
proving something, either to
ourselves or to someone else.

**If you don't start, it's certain
you won't arrive.**

---●---

**What you can't
communicate runs your life.**

If you don't have what you
want, you are not
committed to it 100%.

Your enemy might become
your friend, if you allow
him to be who he is.

If you worry about what
might be, and wonder what
might have been, you will
ignore what is.

Before you can break out of
prison, you must first realize
you're locked up.

When you blame others, you give up your power to change.

Whatever you are willing to put up with is exactly what you will have.

— • —

If you acknowledge you are
unconscious, you are no
longer unconscious.

**Divorces are final long
before they go to court.**

———————— ◆ ————————

Your interpretation of what
you see and hear is just that,
your interpretation.

————————————————

If you find a good solution
and become attached to it,
the solution may become
your next problem.

●

Criticize the performance,
not the performer.

What works for you may
not work for someone else.
So what makes you think
your way is so much better?

---●---

When you really take a good
look at your life, Success is
all you've ever had.

If you are not rich, notice
how you make yourself
poor.

You are the cause of everything that happens to you. Be careful what you cause.

There is no right or wrong,
only consequences.

The one who loves the least
controls the relationship.

If you require someone to change, you require that person to lie to you.

If you don't like the
direction the river is
flowing, don't jump in.

We fear the thing we want
the most.

Feelings of inferiority and
superiority are the same.
They both come from fear.

After all is said and done,
much is said and little is
done.

The biggest risk in life is not
risking.

---●---

What we Are is God's gift to
us. What we Become is our
gift to God.

Excuses are your lack of
faith in your own power.

—————————•—————————

**Things are not what they
seem, they are what they
are.**

—————————

You can get everything in life you want, if you will help enough other people get what they want.

If you don't like the games
people play, make up your
own games.

---•---

There are many things I want, but few things I need.

If you prepare for old age,
old age comes sooner.

If you have a college degree you can be absolutely sure of one thing . . . you have a college degree.

There is brutality and there
is honesty. There is no such
thing as brutal honesty.

---•---

**If you are going to give a
gift, notice your true
intentions.**

There are no victims, only
volunteers.

If you are not leaning, no
one will ever let you down.

People concern themselves
with being normal, rather
than natural.

Ultimately you have no choice but to feel what you are feeling.

If you have made yourself
important, notice you're not
important.

**Worry comes from the belief
you are powerless.**

———————— ● ————————

**Your ability to relax is in
direct proportion to your
ability to trust life.**

———————————

Any system that takes responsibility away from people, dehumanizes them.

———————— ● ————————

**Whatever you want, wants
you.**

Most of the time we don't communicate, we just take turns talking.

We fear the thing we want
the most.

---•---

If you have to be happy you
will always be unhappy.

---- • ----

Nostalgia isn't what it used to be.

---•---

What you are afraid to do is a clear indicator of the next thing you need to do.

If you stick your head in the
sand, one thing is for sure,
you'll get your rear kicked.

If you are honest because
honesty is the best policy,
then your honesty is
corrupt.

———————— • ————————

**Maturity consists of no
longer being taken in by
one's self.**

Once you realize you have given your power away, you can make the decision to take it back.

---- ● ----

**Less effort creates more
results.**

If you have a constant need to help other people, notice how you must keep them helpless.

———————— • ————————

**Life always keeps its
agreement with you.**

There are none so righteous
as the newly converted.

**Hoping and Wishing are
excuses for not Doing.**

The rewards in life go to
those who are willing to give
up the past.

If your life isn't working the
way you want it to, notice
you're lying.

I'm going to be assertive . . .
if that's ok with you!

You are the cause, not the
effect.

Once you accept an idea it's
an idea whose time has
come.

You get treated in life the
way you *train* people to
treat you.

If you are not leaning, no one will ever let you down.

If you let other people do it
for you, they will do it *to*
you.

99% responsibility doesn't
work.

The harder I work the
luckier I get!

There are three kinds of
people: Those who make
things happen, Those who
watch things happen, and
Those who don't know what
the hell is happening!

It's easier to *say* what we believe than *be* what we believe.

———————•———————

**Whatever you resist,
persists.**

---●---

You can love someone and
not like the way they act.

Too often we want justice
. . . just for us.

People who can't face drugs, turn to reality.

God doesn't make faulty
products.

You are never alone with
schizophrenia.

Paradox—if you give up the
need for security, you will be
secure.

If you are afraid to lose anything you have, at some point in your life you will lose it.

---•---

**Defeat comes from solutions
that don't work.**

The way to win is to make it
ok to lose.

Whatever you assume to be
true will become *real* for
you.

Life is what's *coming*, not
what *was*.

Things that come to those who wait may be the things left by those who got there first.

Life is a journey, not a
destination.

You must give up the way it
is . . . to have it the way
you want it.

If you don't change your
beliefs your life will be like
this forever. Is that good
news?

---●---

We move toward what we
picture in our mind.

---•---

**People who believe things
can't be done will go out
and prove they are "right."**

The more investment you
have in your beliefs, the
harder it is to change them.

Hope is what keeps all
suffering in place.

You are the only teacher you
will ever have.

If you don't know what
direction to take, you
haven't acknowledged where
you are.

People would rather be
"right" than be happy.

THINK
AGAIN

———————— ◆ ————————

---•---

Dependency is slavery by
mutual agreement.

If you don't make a choice,
someone else will choose *for*
you.

———————●———————

**Learn to create, not
compete.**

———————————

———————— • ————————

One hundred years from
now, no one will care!

If you don't go within, you
will go without.

Anger is one letter short of danger.

Your success is measured by your ability to complete things.

The more clear you are on
what you want, the more
power you will have.

---●---

Therapists are expensive friends.

———————

The biggest lie on the
planet: "When I get what I
want I will be happy."

---·---

**Yesterday was the deadline
for all complaints.**

There are only two things
you "have to" do in life: You
"have to" die, and you
"have to" live until you die.
You make up all the rest.

Look for opportunity, not
guarantees.

You can be happy *or* you
can be justified. You can't
be *both*.

If you think something outside of yourself is the cause of your problem, you will look outside of yourself for the answer.

Keep the *lesson* but throw
away the *experience*.

When it becomes more
difficult to suffer than
change . . . you will change.

Some people try to softly tiptoe through life so that they can arrive at death safely!

You have mastered life when
the "how to's" are
irrelevant.

Procrastination is the fault
most people put off
correcting.

You will never "have it all together." That's like trying to eat once and for all!

All unhappiness is caused by
comparison.

---•---

**We are the people our
parents warned us about!**

It is not enough to aim, you must hit.

---- • ----

Sickness is faulty problem
solving.

Most advice is worth what it costs: nothing!

---— ● ---—

You lose what you don't use.

**If you and your partner
always agree, one of you is
unnecessary!**

We neither get better or
worse as we get older, but
more like ourselves.

If you want to make an enemy, try to change someone.

There is no security between
the cradle and the grave.

Fortune favors the bold!

Not to decide, is to decide.

———————— ● ————————

You love what you find time
to do.

————————————

Success is getting up one
more time.

When your ship comes in,
make sure you are willing to
unload it.

Some people are dead, but
still moving!

The best way to escape from
your problem is to solve it.

There is no such thing as
smoking in moderation.

Often, believing is seeing.

We weaken whatever we
exaggerate.

What is, was What was, is
What will be, is up to me.

If at first you don't succeed,
you're about average.

—— • ——

Lead, follow, or get out of
the way.

Live as though it were your last day on earth. Some day you will be right!

THINK
AND WIN

———————————•———————————

Winners are *ordinary* people
with *extraordinary*
determination.

———————— • ————————

It doesn't matter what you
can do, what matters is
what you *will* do.

A Winner is always part of
the *answer*. A Loser is
always part of the *problem*.

Winning Formula:
Ability × Effort = Results

You have to *be* before you can *do*, and you have to *do* before you can *have*.

If you can't find the time to
do it right the first time,
when are you going to find
the time to do it over?

Resistance to change is
nothing more than
"hardening of the attitudes."

A Winner must call himself
"great" before the world
does.

Winners never quit. Quitters
never win.

People who achieve true
success rarely worry about
being successful.

Experience is the best
teacher, provided we become
the best students.

The greatest understanding
you can have, if you want to
be enlightened, is that no
one will ever understand
you.

Out of every failure and disappointment is the seed of an *equivalent* or *greater* benefit.

Handicaps are given to
ordinary people to help
them to become
extraordinary.

It is not what you *know* that
gets you into trouble. It's
what you *think you know*,
that isn't so!

The mind is like a
parachute, it works best
when it is open.

The goal of a Winner should be *excellence*—not perfection.

If you are not making 50 mistakes a day, you're not trying hard enough!

You cannot strengthen the
weak by weakening the
strong.

You cannot lead someone to *permanent* change by doing for them what they *can* and *should* do for themselves.

Winning is the result of good judgment. Good judgment is the result of experience.

It's always too soon to quit.

The best way to *predict* your future is to *create* it.

———————●———————

Most people do very efficiently what needs not be done at all.

———————————

---●---

Often, short-term gain
produces long-term pain.

No one "does it to you." You do it to *yourself, through* other people.

Winning is accomplished in the *preparation* phase, not the execution phase.

A Winner says, "It may be difficult, but it's possible." A Loser says, "It may be possible, but it's too difficult."

Guilt is resentment directed
toward *ourselves*.
Resentment is anger directed
toward *others*.

Trying is lying. To *do* is to be true.

Winning requires getting up
off your affirmation.

You will either live up to, or down to, your *self-expectations*.

A Winner believes we make
our own "luck" by what we
do or *fail* to do. A Loser
believes in "good luck" and
"bad luck."

Losers mistake activity for accomplishment. Winners know that accomplishment is the *result* of activity.

You only get what you give
yourself—so give yourself
the best.

Horsesense is nothing more
than having good stable
knowledge.

What you *get* by reaching
your destination is not as
important as what you
become by reaching your
destination.

If your outflow exceeds your inflow, your upkeep will be your downfall.

---•---

Most people fail in life because they *major* in *minor* things.

Losers focus on making a *living*. Winners focus on making a *life*.

---•---

If you don't have a clear
goal in life, you are destined
to work for someone who
does.

It is not enough to *see* the possibility, you must *become* the possibility.

Get very good at what you love to do, because you can never get good enough at something you are not suited for.

A Winner sees an answer in every problem. A Loser just sees the problem.

It is impossible to *win* unless
you *begin*.

Nothing in life *"costs too much."* The truth is *you* can either afford it, or *you* can't.

A relationship is like a gem—it requires friction to polish it.

Marriage can often be
described as two people
agreeing to change each
other's habits.

If you will make the
decision, your subconscious
will make the *provision*.

If you ask for what you want, you will not have to take only what is offered.

Ideas without labor are
stillborn.

One of the things we can do
to help the poor is not to
become one of them!

Stop sweating the small
stuff because, 100 years
from now, no one will care!

A Winner says, "Let's find
out." A Loser says, "Nobody
knows."

Life is a persistent teacher.
It will keep repeating lessons
until we learn.

—————●—————

Illness is the ultimate wake-up call!

Winning requires shifting
emphasis from *won't* power
to *will*power.

I'm going to be assertive, if
that's okay with you!

If you will live as though
every day were your last day
on earth—someday you'll be
right!

If you want to know what your true *beliefs* are—take a look at your *actions*.

You can only reason
someone out of what they
have been reasoned into.

Positive lessons are not always taught in positive ways.

He who gives uninvited
advice first . . . loses.

—————— • ——————

If you argue for your
limitations, you get to keep
them.

——————————

A rebel is a person who conforms to nonconformity.

———— ◆ ————

When you do the things you *need* to do, when you *ought* to do them, the day will come when you can do the things you *want* to do *when* you *want* to do them.

————

A Winner says, "I will!" and succeeds. A Loser says, "I'll try," and fails.

---- • ----

Negative thinking is mental
malpractice.

Wishing is a goal without *energy* behind it.

---- • ----

A Winner is not afraid to
lose. A Loser is secretly
afraid of winning.

The way you are is *not* the
result of what has happened
to you, it's the result of what
you decide to *keep inside* of
you.

Many people try to softly
tiptoe through life so that
they can arrive at death
safely.

Accept nothing without *examination. Reject* nothing without *consideration*.

If you keep *doing* what you have been *doing*, you will keep *getting* what you have been *getting*.

Affirmation without *action*
leads to *delusion*.

Winners do not do
extraordinary things. They
do ordinary things
extraordinarily well.

The ultimate judgment of progress is: *measurable* results in *reasonable* time.

THINK
TOGETHER

———————•———————

You're never going to "have it all together." That's like trying to eat once and for all!

———————— • ————————

**Whatever you are ready for
is ready for you.**

---●---

The only thing worse than talking about others and being a gossip is talking about yourself and being a bore.

─────

A simple truth: It's impossible to be depressed when you take *action*.

---- • ----

Most people are willing to
change, not because they see
the light, but because they
feel the heat.

When your partner is in trouble, don't just ask if there is anything you can do, think of something appropriate and *do* it.

It is not enough to give what
we *have*; we must also give
what we *are*.

---- • ----

You cannot influence your
partner if you are not also
susceptible to influence
yourself.

Don't lead me; I may not follow. Don't walk behind me; I may not lead. Walk beside me and be my friend.

---◆---

The way to truly appreciate
someone is to realize that
you might lose them
someday.

Don't go to bed mad.
Instead, stay up and have a
good fight. Then make up.

---- ◆ ----

**Nothing is as self-blinding
as being self-righteous.**

If you want to persuade
your partner, you must
appeal to interest rather
than to intellect.

Being a true friend is being
interested in others, not
showing them how
interesting you are.

Getting rid of bad habits is
like peeling an onion, it
must be done one layer
at a time.

---●---

Trust eliminates fear.

A Winner makes
commitments. A Loser
makes promises.

———————— ● ————————

It is foolish to punish your
partner by fire when you
live under the same roof.

————————————————

**During trying times, keep
trying.**

Until we are all that *we* wish
to be, how can we be upset
with someone who is not
what we wish them to be?

Learning to be alone and not be lonely means you're ready to be with someone else.

---- ● ----

If I trust you to tell me what
is best for you, I trust you
will know that I know what
is best for me.

────────────

———————•———————

**Believe in yourself first, then
you can believe in another.**

———————•———————

When we focus on solving
problems, we avoid placing
blame.

———————•———————

Showing who we truly are
versus showing who we
think we should be is the
essence of true love.

————————————————

Commitment comes from
the heart; it is not just an
agreement.

It takes two to tangle.

———————— • ————————

Careful word selection is
vitally important in a
relationship—think and
speak from the heart, not
the head.

————————————————

Helping others is the best
way to rid yourself of your
own troubles.

Sticks and stones may break
our bones, but words can
break our hearts.

———————— • ————————

Love lets the past die by
moving us to a new
beginning without changing
the past.

————————————

---•---

**He who gets angry first
usually loses.**

———— ● ————

Kind words can be short
and easy to speak, but their
echoes are truly endless.

Love doesn't make the
world go round. Love is
what makes the ride
worthwhile.

———————————— ● ————————————

Our perception in
relationships is a mirror.

You cannot be friends with anyone else if you are not a friend to yourself.

---●---

Forgiveness is the key to happiness.

———————————— ● ————————————

Relationships take a
commitment to working
together, even when we feel
like we don't want to.

————————————————

Understanding does not
necessarily mean agreement.

Only one response to
conflict can open the door to
intimacy—that is, an intent
to learn from the experience.

The more love we share with
everyone, the more lovable
we become.

—————— ● ——————

If we want peace, we must
give up the idea of conflict
once and for all.

——————————————

No matter how wonderful
love can be, no one person
can meet all our needs.

Your partner is easier to love
when happy. Why not help
your partner to be happy?

Times of withdrawal are as
necessary as times of
intimacy.

Most often our partner
wants us to listen and not
give advice.

The couple that plays
together, stays together.

When resentment slips in,
focus on the good you see in
one another.

Love yourself first, because
you can't give something
you don't already have.

True friends agree to tell
each other things they
wouldn't tell themselves.

Politeness is the oil that
keeps the relationship
machine running smoothly.

You can neither give nor
receive if you are obsessed
with holding on to someone.

---●---

Your partner cannot keep
anything from you that you
haven't kept from yourself.

———————

—————— • ——————

**Being alone with someone
else is the loneliest place in
the world.**

—————————————

There is never too much communication in a relationship; the problems lie with too much at one time.

———————— • ————————

Whatever someone boasts
the most of . . . is what they
are likely to have the least
of.

A person who loves
unconditionally cannot be
controlled.

If you can accept that you are okay the way you are— you can stop trying to prove you're okay.

———— • ————

You will never let yourself
have more love than you
think you deserve.

Tact is knowing how far is
too far to go.

Your self-worth must be
stronger than anyone's
rejection.

If you are not trying to get
something from someone
else, you cannot be
exploited.

The reason it is harder to be
a receiver than a giver is
because a giver is always in
control.

A relationship should be like
a fishing trip, keep the good
stuff and throw the small
stuff back.

If your goal is to get your mate's approval, one thing is for sure—you will never get it.

You cannot lead someone to positive change by doing for them what they *should* be doing for themselves.

Your partner cannot do anything to you that you have not given permission to do.

---•---

**We attract the people we
feel we are worthy of.**

Accept nothing your partner
says without examination,
reject nothing your partner
says without consideration.

In any relationship, you will keep getting what you have been getting until you stop doing what you are doing.

———————— ● ————————

Unhappiness can come from frustration if one side of your life is not being fulfilled. What about your other half?

————————————

---•---

(In a relationship) a
problem shared is a problem
cut down to size.

You are the only one who won't leave you.

There are two sides to
almost every situation;
consider both.

If you don't have love in
your heart, you have the
worst kind of heart trouble.

In any relationship, you will always find what you are looking for.

The road to a successful relationship is always under construction.